Foreword

Memories of Wigan is a compilation of photographs from the not-too-distant past, all with one very important thing in common; they have been chosen according to their ability to rekindle memories of times gone by. Times and events which will be within the lifetime of most readers, and photographs of local places which are certain to evoke feelings of nostalgia in anyone with an interest in Wigan.

The book has relatively modest aims; it is not intended to be a history book, it has much more to do with entertainment than serious study, but if it prompts people to take more interest in the history of their town, then so much the better!

The following pages contain a variety of pictures with subject matter ranging from Royal visits to sporting events, and from 1950s town-centre shopping scenes to pictures of people at work and at play. Wigan at war gets a mention too, with memorable pictures of fund raising and morale-boosting occasions in the town.

We hope that people with a genuine interest in Wigan will be prompted to remember the sights, sounds and even the distinctive aromas of the past by the photographs featured here. If this is the outcome, then we shall have achieved our objective. Compiling Memories of Wigan has been a pleasure. Whatever your age, I hope you enjoy reading it.

Happy memories!

Phil Holland
Publisher.

Wigan Heritage Service

A sunny day and a Royal Visit; what more could any child ask for in October 1954 when the Queen came to town

First published in 1997 by:
True North Books
Dean Clough
Halifax
HX3 5AX
Tel 01422 344344

a
true north
book

Copyright © True North Holdings

Contents

Wigan Heritage Service

The sheer warmth of the occasion when Gracie Fields visited Wigan is captured in this lovely photograph. 'Our Gracie' ranked at the very top of her profession, alongside Wigan's own favourite, George Formby.

Acknowledgments

The publishers would like to thank the following for helping to make this book possible: Wigan Heritage Services, in particular Alastair Gillies and Len Hudson for granting permission to use many old photographs from their archives. Several of the 1954 Royal visit pictures sourced through Wigan Heritage Services were taken from the Reg Tolson Collection and thanks are due to Mr Tolson for allowing us to use them. Thanks are also due to the many local businesses who have allowed us to "tell their story" through the pages of this book and by supporting the title have enabled us to keep the price to a relatively modest level. Finally, thanks also to Gareth Martin for organising the advertising content and to Mandy Walker for her endless patience exercised whilst designing the pages.

Right: Coronation Day in 1937 was a time of tremendous celebration throughout the country, based on widespread genuine affection for the monarchy. This photograph, of sixty years ago, shows the staff of R & J Gorner, the popular Wigan café as they pose for a commemorative picture outside their premises. Even the café mascot made an appearance!

Wigan Heritage Service

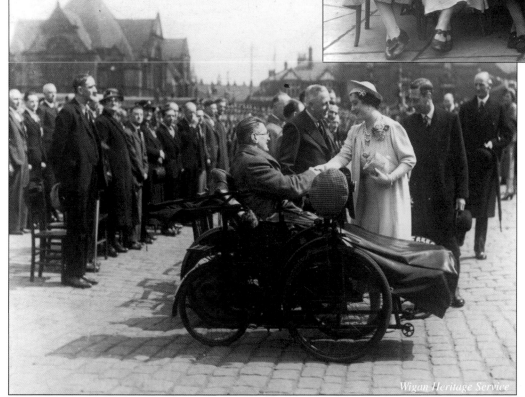

Wigan Heritage Service

Left: Friday May 20th 1938 was the date that this picture was taken in the Market Square. The occasion was a visit by their Majesties King VI and Queen Elizabeth, as part of a wider tour of north west towns and cities. The royal party entered the Borough at the boundary at Warrington Road, progressing through Skew Bridge, Newtown and along Wallgate, Market Street to Market Square. Market day had been brought forward to Thursday to make sure that the spacious Market Square would be available for the visit. School children were given a day's holiday, as were the Corporation's employees, and the Mayor appealed to local businessmen to make the same offer to their workers. As was usual on occasions such as this, a large parade was organised which involved members of the 5th Battalion, The Manchester Regiment, the British Legion, the St. John's Ambulance Brigade. Wigan had been decorated on the instruction of the Corporation by the Borough Engineer's department, and bunting, flags and streamers were displayed to add to the atmosphere of the occasion at every available point along the route. The Parish Church bells peeled from early morning to celebrate the royal visit, and twenty local citizens were presented to their Majesties at the climax of the tour.

Wigan Heritage Service/Reg Tolson collection

The Royal Motorcade slowly moves along Market Street during the Royal Visit of October 1954

Glorious weather met the arrival of the Royal Couple when they visited Wigan on 21st October 1954 and the next four pages includes scenes from their visit. The event was described as 'Wigan's Great Day' in the local press, and, coming just nine short years after the end of the war it is not surprising that the occasion boosted the morale of local people and filled the streets with happy, cheering crowds. This was the first visit to the area of Her Majesty Queen Elizabeth II and H.R.H The Duke of Edinburgh. Everyone made an early start on the day so as not to miss their chance of getting a good view of the popular young couple. School children assembled in their classes long before they normally would, to be given strict instructions about how they were to conduct themselves on the journey into town, and, no doubt, about how important it was to give a good impression of the school throughout the day. Flag sellers and street vendors selling a variety of goods were out in force from early

Wigan Heritage Service/Reg Tolson collection

Crowds in Wallgate cheer the Queen and Prince Philip as they pass

on. Staff set to work in the North Western Station at six in the morning and performed a transformation of the grey interior to make it literally fit for Royalty. Acres of red carpet, flags, bunting and flowers were put in place; all was made ready for the ten o'clock arrival of the Royal train.

In the event, the train was slightly early, and the tension mounted as onlookers in the station saw the silhouette of the young queen and her taller husband preparing to step out of the carriage and onto the platform. The door of the eighth carriage, perfectly aligned with the crimson carpet so carefully laid, slowly opened and the Royal couple became visible for the first time. The Queen, smiling broadly, stepped forward to be greeted by the Lord Lieutenant, the Earl of Derby M.C and the Countess. Cheers rang out spontaneously from the gathering in the station. Introductions followed, including those to the Mayor and Mayoress, Cllr and Mrs T.S Merry, the Chief Constable and other local dignitaries.

A sea of smiling faces lined Wallgate as the Queen's car moved off from the railway station

Wigan Heritage Service/Reg Tolson

In the background the flashes of photographers cameras could be seen, and a top-hatted cine camera operator could be seen manoeuvring discreetly in order to find the best angles for his shots. The Queen was wearing a smoke-blue fitted A-line coat with an amethyst-sequinned collar and matching hat. The Duke looked sun-tanned and handsome in a dark grey lounge suit, with hands characteristically clasped behind his back as he walked, smiling through the Wigan crowds. The Royal party made its way through the station subway, down the carpeted steps and along the walkway which by now was decorated by the huge drapings of red, white and blue. As they moved onto the station forecourt a huge burst of sunlight and deafening cheers greeted them. Meanwhile, along Wallgate, people had, by now been waiting from 7 or 8.00am to catch their glimpse of the Royal visitors. The crowd was ten or twelve deep in places, and were being controlled, if that is the word, by hundreds of police, soldiers, and even

Wigan Heritage Service/Reg Tolson collection

Standing room only along Market Square, awaiting the arrival of the Queen's party in October 1954

fire brigade personnel. Mounted policemen patrolled the route that the royal party was to take, clattering noisily up and down the cobbled roadways, urging the adults in the crowd to keep the enthusiastic children back from the roadside. By now, people were looking for vantage points; office windows above street-level were crammed with eager faces, high, often precarious vantage points were scaled by the athletic and ingenious in order to find that ideal spot from which to secure an ideal view. Soon the waiting was rewarded. Her Majesty's gleaming black Rolls Royce, plumed with the royal standard and supported by four other immaculately turned out vehicles, all travelling at a sedate 2 miles per hour was soon travelling to the John McCurdy Hall, and the main purpose of the visit. Along the route the policemen fought to keep the enthusiastic supporters back, unsuccessfully in some cases, as the eager crowds spilled from the pavement onto the road.

Overhead keen ears could just about make out the sound of a light aircraft, manned by police officers and tasked with monitoring the progress of the royal motorcade as it crawled through Wigan. The airborne observers were linked, by radio, to a set on the handlebars of a B.S.A motorcycle being ridden by the officer in charge of the police escort below; quite an innovation for the time. By this time, the police estimated that around 100,000 people were on the streets of Wigan to welcome their monarch to the town.

The cars soon arrived at the John McCurdy Hall. It had been opened at a cost of £220,000, with further additions planned which would bring the total up to more than a million pounds. Local dignitaries were introduced to the Queen and Prince Philip, and a special conversation took place with Cllr McCurdy, the hard working civic figure after whom the building had been named. A gold key was presented to the Queen who used it to open a door and formally declare the building open.

Above: The Silver Jubilee year of Her Majesty Queen Elizabeth II was 1977, and Wigan, like many towns and cities, was honoured by a visit from the Monarch. This was the first royal visit to the area since 1954, and, when Her Majesty stepped out of the North West Station she was met by the Mayor, Councillor Tom Morgan, and the ringing cheers of ten thousand loyal subjects. The Queen was dressed in a turquoise A-line coat with matching straw hat. Appropriately the royal train was driven by a Wigan man, Mr Arthur Robinson of Ruskin Drive. The Queen called at Wigan as part of her two day tour of the north west; it was a short visit before she went on to Leigh. A local newspaper report from the time described how a local lady, Mrs Helen Ratcliffe of Abram had managed to speak with the Queen; 'it was the greatest moment of my life... I'll never forget this day' she said. Her Majesty is seen here on the dais with the guard of honour which was provided by the Duke of Lancaster's own Yeomanry. Earlier in the year there was controversy in Wigan when the Council reversed a decision to provide a free commemorative mug for the town's schoolchildren. The gift would have cost the town £20,000 which worked out at 34p per mug. In the end the Council decided that the money could be better spent elsewhere and the mugs were never purchased.

Wigan Heritage Service/Reg Tolson collection

The Queen and Prince Philip about to officially open the John McCurdy Hall

A glorious summer day in Mesnes Park, was the setting for this delightful photograph which dates from the 1920s. The tree-covered river embankment can be seen in the distance, but all eyes and ears in this scene are focussed clearly on the music being played in the bandstand. Note the distinctive fashions from the time; the ladies look so stylish in their long coats and distinctive hats, you can really feel the atmosphere of the day when you study the picture. The photograph was taken from an elevated position, above the bandstand, from the café that is located there. Outdoor concerts were very popular in Mesnes Park in the days before television and the widespread ownership of wireless sets. Most people of the day would have been regular church-goers, and entertainment would have been sought within walking distance of home, or at the most, a short tram journey in the days before motoring was commonplace.

Below: A family scene captured in the late 1950s in Mesnes Park. In the background the popular café can be seen on its elevated mound. Perhaps the family featured in the picture was just returning from there. We shall never know. Remember elaborate coachbuilt prams like the one shown here? Many mothers would take the kind of pride in their prams that people today take in their cars! Mesnes park was ideal for an outing with a baby, endless smooth footpaths, birds singing in the trees and only the distant murmur of traffic from the adjacent roads. Wonderful!

Above: A tranquil scene. Three children gaze into the quiet waters which characterise this part of the facility in one of the jewels in the crown of Wigan's public facilities. The well kept park, which is only a short walk from the hustle and bustle of the town centre, has provided local people with a veritable oasis of peace and harmony since it opened over a century ago.

Wigan Heritage Service

Right: A rare aerial view of Mesnes Park showing the layout of the park in almost map-like detail. The well used café on its slightly raised mound can be seen just below the centre of the picture, and below that, to the right, is the bandstand which has been the focus of so many concerts over the years. It may just be possible to make out the statue of Sir Francis Sharp Powell, at the side of the main path running almost vertically down the park. It was erected in 1910. Bridgeman Terrace can be seen on the left hand side of the park - known by local people as *Park View* . At the bottom left of the picture Rylands Mill is visible, and at the opposite corner the distinctive outline of Wigan Grammar School is shown.

Below, and below right: The date of origin of these two photographs is not precisely known, but they show people enjoying some fairground activities on Mesnes Park. Yet another past function of the highly prized local facility in days gone by.

Wigan Heritage Service

Wigan Heritage Service

Wigan Heritage Service

Wigan Town Centre was the venue for Wigan's annual carnival for many years. This picture dates from the late 1940s and shows Wiganers in celebratory mood.

Not the most politically correct photograph in the book, but interesting nevertheless. This 1950s picture shows a crowd of onlookers waiting at the roadside for one of Wigan's Carnival Processions.

Another busy scene in the town centre showing a troupe of 'clowns' marching to the enjoyment of hundreds of onlookers. Note the fact that virtually all the people seen here are wearing hats - entirely typical of the time. Some of the shops seen here will be familiar names to many readers: Latimer's Grocers, Turner's Footwear and Bradley's the outfitters will bring back memories of shopping days in the past.

Right: Munitions workers from Beech Hill pose for a photograph on the steps leading up to the café at Mesnes Park. The people seen here are mainly young women, as you expect, and they are seen here with some examples of their work, shell cases for the 'twenty-five pounders' which were made at the purpose built factory. Some of the workers at Beech Hill were evacuees from the parts of Britain most affected by the German air raids. The workers are looking in the direction of Wigan Parish Church and the town centre in this photograph, over the roof of the old Wigan Grammar School. Behind the group, and in front of the café is the monument to the local men who served in the South African War. The pedestal remains there to this day, the inscription reading: *This Memorial was erected by public subscription to the memory of the men belonging to the Regular Volunteer and Imperial Yeomanry Forces of Wigan and district who fell in the South African War, 1899-1902.*

Wigan Heritage Service

Far left: Burneys handbag factory as it was in this pre-World War II photograph showing just how labour-intensive the production process was at the time. Almost a hundred lady operatives can be seen, each with a specific role to play in the manufacture of the highly prized accessories, and, in the distance the stern production foremen in their white coats look on. Of course, virtually every supervisor or foreman was male in those days as employers had a very blinkered view of the abilities of women in the workplace. Burneys made stylish handbags at their factory on Woodhouse Lane for many years, providing much needed employment in Wigan. *Left:* This picture showing P.C Lowe of the Wigan Police dates from 1957. In the days before personal radios it could be a real problem keeping in touch with officers on their beat, and these police telephone points were an attempt at improving the situation. Strategically placed around the town, a light on top would flash to attract the attention of a passing policeman so that he could be directed to where he was needed most. The public could also use a handset in the box in order to call '999'.

Wigan Heritage Service

Jones & Park: Quality clothing in Wigan since 1924

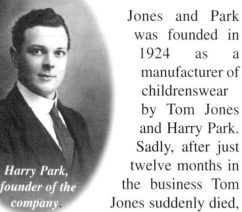

Harry Park, founder of the company.

Jones and Park was founded in 1924 as a manufacturer of childrenswear by Tom Jones and Harry Park. Sadly, after just twelve months in the business Tom Jones suddenly died, leaving Harry Park to develop the company alone.

Throughout the years of the depression, growth was extremely gradual but sustained, and by the time of the Second World War, the company was granted 'Designated Status' enabling it to continue, throughout the war

years, to produce much needed clothing.

Indeed this was so important that the company's bank offered to store the valuable fabrics in their vaults to protect them against potential bomb damage!

A man keen on sport, indeed he was a water polo goal keeper, Harry Park was very strong. Unfortunately his health had suffered since contracting trench fever during the First World War and sadly he died in 1949.

The original premises in Rowbottom Square, in the centre of Wigan, were beginning to prove expensive and inefficient. They consisted of two buildings and four floors, and so in

1970, the company moved to a single storey building in Sharp Street, Wallgate, which had previously housed Victoria Ward Labour Club.

This street no longer exists, it is now the site of Wigan Motor Company. Jones and Park is now located in a modern, purpose built sewing factory on the corner of Wilcock Street and Miry Lane at Wallgate Industrial Estate. The company took over these premises in 1983.

position of having to compete with each other, their desire for their own identity increases. This is just one of a many reasons why Jones and Park expect to be in Wigan for the celebration of their centenary in the year 2024.

The photographs on these pages were kindly supplied by Jones and Park and show various rooftop views of Wigan around the Market Place area, taken in the late 1920s.

The company is still run by the descendants of Harry Park. The company is wholly owned by his daughters and grandchildren and his grandson is in control.

The company specialise in childrenswear, concentrating nowadays entirely on girl's school uniforms.

Everything is made to order and to the specification required by the individual schools. Although the company supplies many state schools, the majority of their customers are world famous names including Roedean, Benenden, Cheltenham Ladies

College, Norland Nannies College, Jersey College for Girls and many more.

The traditional school outfitters still exist through the larger department stores of John Lewis branches and Harrods and through the many privately owned high street retailers throughout the United Kingdom and Channel Islands.

Most traditionalists will agree that it is good to know that the British institution of *school uniforms* is still alive. As schools are now almost in the

Rathbones - Perfect bread that's been over 100 years in the making

The history of Rathbones bakery goes back to before the turn of the century, when Mr Alfred Rathbone, at the age of 18, opened a general goods stall in Wigan Market in 1879. He followed this by moving to Newtown to open a grocery shop a few years later, at which his sons, Sydney, Tom and Jack baked bread for customers in the locality.

This was the scenario just before the outbreak of the First World War, when all three sons joined the army. Naturally enough, for the duration the business was placed on hold. Luckily at the cessation of hostilities the three brothers were able to return to Wigan unharmed apart from Sydney who received a severe dose of mustard gas which affected him for many years. The bread being baked was proving so popular that the young men decided to move to new premises in Bridgewater Street. Looking to the future, it was decided to purchase horse drawn bread vans to supply other customers in the locality.

Motorised vehicles were introduced for the first time in 1920, followed by more new bakery premises in 1921, later to become the company's present Newtown site, off the Warrington Road.

Fire

In 1936 a fire at the laundry premises, immediately adjacent to the bakery enabled the business to expand again after purchasing the burnt out site. 1938 saw the introduction of the first automatic bread oven with supporting machinery. This oven gave service for 35 years before being replaced. During the war years the lack of wrapping paper and packaging did not permit wrapped and sliced bread production. However, in 1945 paper became available, allowing bread slicing and wrapping to resume. It was an immediate success. With Mr Sydney's dedication to producing quality products, demand grew so much that an additional bread plant was introduced in 1948, followed soon after in 1954 by a third production line.

Conventional dough making methods until then had been the order of the day, using the three hour fermentation process. However, in the early 1960s high speed mixing using the Chorleywood process became more and more popular with the company's competitors. Reluctantly Rathbones followed suit in 1967. It turned out to be wise decision, as product quality was greatly improved.

In 1950 Mr Sydney's son, Tom joined the business, both working closely together for many years, enabling Sydney to pass on his knowledge to a future generation of bakers. In addition to learning

accommodation. At this time bag flour was replaced by the installation of four twenty- ton silos followed shortly afterwards by two fifty-ton silos.

Confectionery

In 1971 the purchase of 15,000 sq ft of land enabled the confectionery side of the business to be developed in which Roger Rathbone, Tom's brother, played a major part. Also, congestion in the despatch and van sales areas resulted in negotiations with the British Legion taking place with the princely sum of £20,000 being paid for two acres of land! Superb, heated despatch and loading bays were then constructed.

The period up to the present day has seen Rathbones products being sold in major food retailers throughout the North and Midlands. With companies such as the Co-operative Societies, Morrisons, Asda and Sainsbury's being worthy of particular note.

The bakery is now owned by the Kear Group, also a family business based in Gloucestershire who are keen to maintain the high standards of quality and service. Rathbones success

was founded upon the dedication of all concerned to maintain consistent quality and excellent service to customers. Only the very best ingredients are used with forward looking progressive developments taking place within the company to combine modern methods with all the virtues of the past.

Facing page, far left: The original premises of Rathbones. This picture dates from the late 1800s.
Facing page, lower picture: A distinctive "3D" advertisement hoarding from the 1950s, promoting the virtues of Rathbones tasty loaves.
Below left: A procession of early 1960s cars passes another Rathbones advertisement hoarding on the outskirts of Wigan.
Left: Two bakery workers in the 1940s.
Below: A group of Wigan Boy Scouts enjoying Rathbones bread in the 1970s.

from his father, Tom Jnr spent nearly three years studying Bakery subjects at Blackpool Technical College. He soon realised that sales were vital to success, but in spite of a certain degree of scepticism from some of the more senior members of his family, he extended the distribution area to include Merseyside, with the first four bread rounds allocated being Ormskirk 1,2,3 and 4, prompting comments from his elders that sales were certainly booming in Ormskirk!

1969 saw the construction of vehicle workshops for complete service and van painting, followed by the building of new office

"Sweet success" for famous Wigan confectionery pioneers...

William Santus and Company have been making quality sweets for almost a century. Their position in this competitive industry is an achievement in itself, but what is more remarkable about Wm Santus and Co is the almost legendary status which has been built up around their 'Uncle Joe's Mint Balls'. Immortalised in countless articles and cartoons there has even been a song written about them! They are synonymous with the town of their production, having gained enormous popularity there since their creation. That town is, of course, Wigan.

Poverty

The founder of the company, William Santus was born on July 27th 1873, and like so many Wiganers of that era, grew up in poverty, as one of seven children. His father worked as a shotfirer in a local colliery and was no stranger to hard work, to say the least. Little is known of William's childhood, except that he left school at fourteen to work for an unknown employer. In 1898 he bought his own fruit stall in the New Market Hall in Wigan and would have probably continued in his chosen line of business had he not met and married Ellen Seddon. The Seddon family had an acquaintance with a family by the name of Atty. The Attys were a family of established confectioners and it was most likely they who taught Ellen Seddon the skillful art of making toffee.

Making toffee began as a sideline on William's fruit stall but Ellen must have showed great aptitude because a few years later they became William's sole product in trade.

By 1908 William had market stalls not only in Wigan but in Bolton and St Helens. The sweets produced were proving immensely popular, and with business thriving Ellen's tiny kitchen was overloaded. William realised that it was time to expand and so the 'Swinley Confectionery Company' was born. William and Ellen went into partnership with William's brother-in-law,

JJ Fortune. In the shadow of the huge Rylands Cotton Mill on a plot of land owned by Mr Fortune, a small domestic factory was built on land where the company would produce its Mint Balls and Treacle Toffee amongst other products.

The sweets were transported to Wigan Market by means of a small truck and the assistance of a young boy called Eric. He had the job of every schoolboy's dreams, hand wrapping the toffees for a 'few bob' a week - and as many sweets as he could eat!

By 1919, demand for the company's products led to the construction of a new factory at Dorning Street, off Wallgate. This move was to be their last, as the company is still there today. When Mr Fortune left the business, the name of the company was changed to William Santus and Company.

MEET UNCLE JOE

Jolly Old Sport is Uncle Joe. He knows what the kiddies like. That is why he never fails to have a supply of Mint Balls.

The Kiddies know this and look forward to Uncle Joe's Mint Balls—an old favourite sweetmeat which always freshen the palate.

Of course the Kiddies put it differently—they say "They're a treat"—Mother says "They're fine for keeping the Kiddies warm and easing the Wheeze."

Get a supply and keep them handy. They are sold everywhere.

8 for a Penny.

UNCLE JOE'S MINT BALLS

6ᴅ PER ½lb TIN

Production increased and more workers were employed and as one of the criteria for gaining employment with the company was that they had to know someone who already worked there, the atmosphere was always friendly and happy.

Mr Santus was the sole managing director and continued to work on the production lines almost until the time of his death in 1953. His speciality was treacle toffee, and his recipe is still one of the biggest sellers to date.

Patent

The 1930s were possibly the most significant in the firm's history. 1933 saw the official patenting of Uncle Joe's Mint Balls and in 1937 the company became fully registered.

Success seemed inevitable, but something was to happen which would cast a cloud over more than the toffee works, the impending outbreak of the Second World War. The introduction of rationing in 1940 could have caused great problems for the company but records show that in fact it made little difference.

What was more threatening was the demand on manpower. Men were being called up to fight for their country and the women to work in the munitions factories in and around the area.

In 1942 the only remaining sugar boiler was called up, forcing Mr Santus to write to the Ministry of Labour, pleading for a 'stay' so that he could train up one of the women to do the job. It was granted.

Incidentally, anyone at school in the Wigan area in 1952 may recall receiving a mug of sweets to commemorate the Queen's Coronation. William Santus were commissioned to make 19,400 ounces of soft centre fruits to be given to all school-children between the ages of 5 and 11.

The way mint-balls are made today is exactly the same as Ellen Santus made them in her tiny kitchen. The only difference is in the wrapping which, today is done by machine. The exact recipe is a closely guarded secret, known only to the current managing directors, Antony and John Winnard.

In the years preceding his death, William Santus had been living in Southport, visiting the factory every morning in his chauffeur driven Daimler. He and Ellen had only one daughter, Nellie, who died on his birthday in 1956, aged only 51. His wife survived

him by ten years, and on her death in 1964 the control of the company passed to her nephew, Frank Winnard.

And so it has remained a family business, with Frank Winnard's grandsons taking over the helm after their father's untimely death in 1990.

Today, Antony and John Winnard employ many local people. The company is as strong as ever, producing sixty different kinds of sweets a year with the most popular product, Uncle Joe's Mint Balls being distributed further and further afield. Chocolates and toffees come and go but the appeal of this historic sweet lives on. How many Wiganers at the turn of the century would have believed that the delicious minty sweet would become such a widely known legend?

Facing page, left: William Santus built this market stall with his own hands. Trays of toffee were broken up with a hammer, with the treacle toffee needing an especially good "crack". *Facing page, right:* The Wigan carnival wouldn't have been complete without the Santus float, dishing out free toffees along the way! *This page, above left:* Another van load of Uncle Joe's Mint Balls is loaded up. *Left:* A favourite picture of Mr Santus, taken in the late 1930s. *Above:* An early advertisement showing a half-pound tin of Uncle Joe's Mint Balls at sixpence a tin. *Right:* Uncle Joe himself, a familiar face to Wigan folk for generations!

Standish Engineering Co Ltd - Precision Engineers since 1951

business progressed, took on four men. At this point Walter Wagstaff decided to join them, and they moved to a single-storey building at St Maries Church, Standish.

Work was secured from the Atomic Energy Authority in the early days of both Windscale and Dounray.

In February 1958 land was purchased from the NCB on the site of the Broomfield Colliery in Bradley Lane, and the first unit of the present factory was erected.

Jack Pyke sadly died of leukaemia in November 1959, and John Hooper and Walter Wagstaff were in partnership when the company was incorporated in 1961.

John Hooper retired from the business in 1986 and it continued to be run by his son, Tony, son in law, Chris Kindon and Walter Wagstaff's son, Peter.

Standish Engineering Co. Ltd., has always taken pride in the quality of its work and the service it provides to its many customers, both locally and nationally. This was recognised in October 1987 by being one of the first companies in the area to be awarded the Quality Award BS 5750, now ISO 9000.

The company has always had a policy of re-investing in the future by continually upgrading and replacing machinery to maintain a competitive edge. In 1994 a further change took place when Peter Wagstaff sold his interest in the business to the other two directors. They continue to manage the business according to the original ideals of a quality subcontracting service with all the advantages of a modern CNC workshop.

Left: A group photograph taken outside the Standish Engineering premises, known as the Mayflower Works, in 1959.

Below: The same premises, in a picture also dating from 1958.

The company was founded by John Reddicliffe Hooper, a Devonian by birth who was sent up to Wigan with eleven other men early in 1939 to create a munitions factory at Bradley Hall, Standish.

It was here that he met, and later married a Wigan girl called Jennie Lawrenson, whose family came from Ince and had a mineral water business.

Standish Engineering Co. was founded in July 1951 with Jackie Pyke with whom John had worked at *Triangle Valve*, on machines rented from Walter Wagstaff.

The venture started in a barn at Graham Farm in Pepper Lane, Standish, initially doing work only for Triangle Valve. They then began to receive work from Electro Hydraulics in Warrington, and, as

Standish Engineering Co Ltd
Precision Engineers

Standish Engineering Co Ltd is a family business which has been established in Wigan for nearly 50 years and is now run by the second generation.

The company offers a high quality sub-contract machining facility which is competitively priced, with deliveries matched to customers individual requirements.

Standish Engineering Co Ltd can proudly offer a spread of very late CNC machines to satisfy most requirements and enquiries. With the company's wide range of capacities covering conventional 2 axis, through to the latest generation sub-spindle bar feed machines, chucking machines with both 2 axis and 4 axis movement and chuck capacities up to 375mm diameter, complemented by a family of machining centres ranging from the rapid 'drill and tap' type to the latest heavyweight twin pallet machines, all rigorously maintained to produce to ever more demanding tolerance and surface finishing requirements.

The firm is proud to have been one of the first companies in the area to be recognised with the Quality Award BS 5750 in October 1987. Now superseded by BS EN ISO 9002.1994, Standish Engineering offers its customers a quality assured service, complimented by the latest CMM technology.

Mayflower Works, Bradley Lane, Standish, Nr Wigan, Lancashire WN6 0XF
Telephone: 01257 422838 Fax: 01257 422381

This Sporting Life

A sea of fans are seen concentrating on the game at Central Park in this picture which was taken on April 7th 1950. The match taking place was against St.Helens. Wigan won, with a scoreline of 17 to 12, with tries by Mountford, Nordgreen and W.Blan, and goals by Ryan.

The decision to build Central Park was taken at a meeting at the turn of the century. The meeting took place in Wigan Public Hall in 1902. The club's roots can be traced back to 1872 when members of Wigan Cricket club got together and drew up plans for organised matches. The first match was played in 1872, when men from the newly formed club played against each other on Folly Field, Upper Dicconson Street. The first competitive match was played against Warrington in January 1873; it ended in a draw.

Wigan experienced one of the greatest periods in their history during a seven year period between 1945 and 1952. The media was packed with news and information about the club; in rugby league terms no other club came close to Wigan at the time and local, national and regional newspapers had an insatiable appetite for stories. During the seven year period Wigan's performance on the field was remarkable, and this was reflected in the number of trophies which were brought back to Central Park. The League Cup was won four times; the Challenge Cup was won twice, and the Lancashire cup was won four times in succession. Their success was attributed to their superior ball handling, and a near telepathic series of relationships between players on the field resulting in a level of fluency that was in a different class to rival clubs.

As you would expect, all this success brought with it a level of support which was the envy of virtually every other rugby league club. Crowds averaged around 22,000 people per home match, with big matches attracting as many as 42,000 supporters.

Wigan Heritage Service

Team talk 1930s style; Harry Sunderland, pictured holding the ball here, was a well known Australian rugby administrator and manager who had successfully led two Australian touring teams in the U.K. Sunderland took over from the even better known George Taylor who retired due to ill health in January 1938. On his retirement the club honoured Taylor by making him a life member of the club and agreeing to pay him a pension of £1 per week. The association between Harry Sunderland and Wigan Rugby League Club was not an entirely happy one by all accounts. The Australian was signed up on a much higher salary than the one paid to the popular George Taylor and there were obvious differences in the way the two parties were used to working. Eventually the parties agreed to part company, and Sunderland left the club in late 1939.

ORRELL RUFC

Edgehall Road, Orrell, Nr Wigan WN5 8TL

Tel 01695 632114 Fax 01695 632116

If you thought Orrell RUFC was just about rugby....

Facilities and location make Orrell an ideal setting for a variety of events. Set in acres of grounds with ample secure parking, Orrell is a perfect place for that special day. Be it a wedding or anniversary, a fund raising event, a private party or company event, Orrell RUFC can offer facilities for 10 to 250 people.

The recently refurbished Clubroom is one of the most desirable venues in the Wigan area. The excellent catering service can provide for all your requirements and you are always guaranteed a warm and friendly reception at competitive rates.

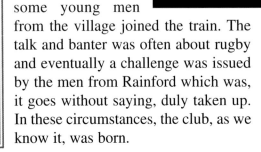

Orrell RUFC - a rugby tradition for 70 years

Precision ball control thanks to a human pyramid!

It is difficult to imagine that Orrell RUFC was once so little known that *The Times* actually managed to misspell the club's name quite regularly, coming up with such distortions as 'Aural', 'Horrel', 'Orl' and 'Oriel' to name but a few!

Orrell was founded in 1927 by a group of friends from Orrell and neighbouring Pemberton, who travelled daily by train to Liverpool. One of the stops on that journey was at Rainford where some young men from the village joined the train. The talk and banter was often about rugby and eventually a challenge was issued by the men from Rainford which was, it goes without saying, duly taken up. In these circumstances, the club, as we know it, was born.

In those early days, the club led a very nomadic existence, with grounds in Kitt Green, Orrell Mount, Abbey Lakes, Alma Hill and Up Holland. Men could be seen most Saturdays carrying rugby posts and sawdust to mark out the pitch in one locality or another, before they eventually settled at the YMCA cricket ground in Winstanley Road.

The Second World War forced the suspension of the club's activities, but as soon as the hostilities had ceased Orrell RUFC was reconstituted. With rapid growth in playing membership, a new ground was sought. The present site at Edge Hall Road was purchased, an ex-army hut being used as changing accommodation in those early days.

Orrell soon developed a reputation on the field that was as much respected as it was feared but improvements in the fixtures list were not easily secured, as they were told by side after side that they would play, but only if others played them also.

In 1971/72 they won the resurrected Lancashire Cup without conceding a point, which also qualified them to take part in the next season's National Knockout Competition (now the Pilkington Cup). In the second round they defeated the famous Harlequins and received wide press coverage, most of the papers managing to spell their name correctly!

From these early days the club has gone from strength to strength, reaching the National Cup quarter and semi finals on a number of occasions. They were an ever present in the English First Division for ten years and finished runners up to Bath in 1991/92.

The club has always built its strength on its commitment to junior rugby and bringing players up 'through the ranks', many of whom played for the

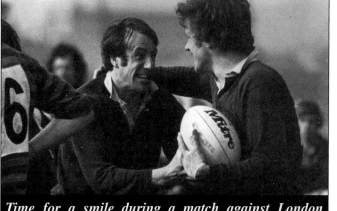

Time for a smile during a match against London Scottish in 1974

first team and achieved representative honours.

On the international stage Frank Anderson, Peter Williams, Fran Clough, Dave Cusani and Nigel Heslop have represented England, John Carleton and Dewi Morris have also played for the British Lions and Simon Mason has represented Ireland.

The advent of the professional game has hit the club hard, losing sixteen of their first team squad before a ball was ever kicked. Not being a club to put themselves in financial difficulties, Orrell have recruited within their means and have brought together a relatively talented but young and inexperienced side. Peter Angelsea has represented England 'A', both Rob Hitchmough and Michael Worsley have played for the England U21 side and Rob Hitchmough and Jim Naylor have

been called up for England Sevens training.

Although their young side played some good rugby and had shown considerable improvement by the end of the 1996/97 season, their lack of experience resulted in their relegation to the Second Division; thereby ending a proud record of having been ever present in the First Division since leagues began.

The spirit amongst the players and coaching staff is high and there is a strong belief that the situation can be turned around and the side get back to winning ways with promotion to the First Division an urgent, essential priority.

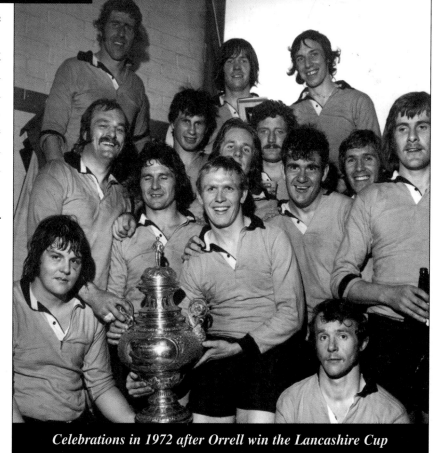

Celebrations in 1972 after Orrell win the Lancashire Cup

Around the Town Centre

This lovely old photograph records a hive of activity on Market Square, with charabancs lined up to take their excited passengers away to the coast. Whether the occasion was an annual Wakes holiday, or a Bank holiday is uncertain. After the war there was a steady increase in the popularity and, for most people, the affordability of holidays and day trips, and thousands of working people would take advantage of the economical, locally-organised trips to get some well earned rest and relaxation. Facing Market Square the red brick building known as the 'gas showrooms' can be seen, and to the right, the old bus station and the buildings beside it which have now been demolished. The sea of cobbles which formed the the Market Square have, sadly, long gone; they found use as much more than a market area over the many years they laid here, and are now covered by the Galleries Shopping Centre.

Wigan Heritage Service

Right: A 1950s view of Standishgate showing shoppers and passers-by seemingly oblivious to the photographer who must have been working at a slightly elevated position. These, in my mind, are always the best record of life in times gone by; much better than most of the posed pictures that have survived the test of time. It is a pity that more of the people featured here are looking away from the camera - but you can't have everything!

Below: This view of Standishgate probably dates from the early 1930s. Note the spoked spare wheel on the motorcar parked just in front of the camera. The Parish Church can just be made out to the right of centre in the distance. Several of the buildings on the right of the scene were demolished around thirty years after the picture was taken. Wiganers may remember the Gas and Electricity company showrooms on the right of the picture lower down the street.

Wigan Heritage Service

Wigan Heritage Service

A delightful view across the rooftops to Haigh, taken from the clock tower of the Parish Church in 1948.

The sign on Victoria House belonging to Lowe's the department store people can just be made out, and the names of the retailers on the other side of the street, including Stylo, Pearl Assurance, Martins Bank, Maypole Dairies, Lace's and Hunter's Grocers are clearly visible too.

The Ritz, with its distinctive angular facade can be seen as you follow the road round to the right. The double-decker bus nearest to the camera is setting passengers down next to the public toilets which remained at this location for several decades after this scene was recorded. Beyond the town-centre shopping area dozens of rows of terraced houses can be seen. Of course, many of those streets have disappeared now. On the right of the picture, in the distance, the spire of St. Catherine's church points skyward. It is a sobering thought to consider that this scene relates to a time only three years after the end of the Second World War. Rationing was still in force on many daily household items and, on the political front, the railways and electricity industries were about to be nationalised; the coal industry had been taken into public ownership during the preceding twelve months.

The year 1948 also saw the creation of the National Health Service in Britain. Certainly the Wigan people in this photograph would have had a lot to occupy their minds when the picture was taken!

Wigan Heritage Service

Wigan Heritage Service

A 1940s view of a wet Market Street shows many of the businesses which were located there. Peter Conroy, the wholesale fruit merchant, and above those premises WH Pennington, the accountant, insurance agent and rent/debt collection agency is based. The offices of the Royal Co-operative Collecting Society are further along the street, and keen-eyed observers may just be able to make out the distinctive sign denoting a pawnbrokers establishment on the other side of the street. The view of the slippery road surface shown here prompts a mention of the level of road traffic accidents in Wigan in the 1940s. The growth in the number of cars outpaced the quality and quantity of the nations' roads and, remember, there were no motorways or by-passes either in those days. On top of this the quality of brakes and tyres on the vehicles of the day, plus the lack of really effective driving tuition, road lighting and layout, resulted in a level of serious road accidents many times the number experienced today.

This view, looking down Library Street records a scene from daily life in the 1950s. The buildings on the left of the picture will be familiar to the Wigan people of today, with one or two exceptions; The Pavilion Cinema at the bottom of the street was a favourite haunt for local folk seeking entertainment, and was noted for its distinctive white facade. It was closed in the late 1950s and the site was used as the location for the new swimming baths. People may be surprised to learn that the light coloured building on the left was a car showroom when this picture was taken, it may just be possible to make out the words 'Austin Automobiles' on the fascia sign. Another element of the street which may bring back a memory or two is the style of the street lighting shown here. It is surprising, initially, just how much of a town's character may be shaped by the 'street furniture' in use in a particular era.

Wigan Heritage Service

One of the most-photographed parts of Wigan, this area of Wallgate with the Parish Church and the elaborate war memorial just in view between the buildings. This photograph dates from the 1950s. The Post Office can be seen on the left, alongside the public house which was later to become the 'Bees Knees'. The war memorial itself dates from 1925, it was designed by Sir Giles Gilbert Scott and unveiled by Sir Herbert A Lawrence in October of the same year. The premises behind the motorcar featured here are occupied, at the time of writing, by a Bookmakers.

Wigan Heritage Service

Market Place in 1954. We can be certain of the date from which the photograph originates because the Transport Offices on the first floor of the building featured here are lavishly decorated. This was done for the visit to Wigan of Queen Elizabeth and the Duke of Edinburgh. The interesting vehicles in the picture add to the 1950s atmosphere, especially the three-wheeled lorry on the right of the scene which would have been a familiar sight on Wigan's roads at the time. In the year that this picture was taken there was a lot going on in the world which would have occupied the minds of the people of Wigan; food rationing came to an end this year and the popular music charts were ringing to the sound of Bill Haley and the Comets' *We're Gonna Rock around the Clock'*. Overseas, Senator McCarthy was embarking on the infamous televised anti-Communist Senate hearings which shook America and had reverberations which were felt throughout the rest of the world. 1954 was also the year that British student Roger Bannister ran the mile in under four minutes, an achievement that boosted the morale of everyone in the country.

MARKET PLACE, WIGAN

L 6266

Wigan Heritage Service

This charming view of Market Place Wigan dates from the late 1950s and is sure to bring back memories of local people who were around during that era. The picture contains many well-loved landmarks, though it has seen many subtle changes over the years. Older residents may remember the time when the road here was a sea of cobbles, punctuated only by the tram lines which carried the trams as they clattered up and down this busy part of the town. On the left of the picture is the rectangular shape described by the railings around the top of the public lavatories which were located deep under the street. The facilities remained there until the mid 1980s. In the centre of the photograph the distinctive Burton's building can be seen, and next to it, on the right, is the building which used to house F.W. Woolworths. The atmosphere is complemented by half a dozen or so 1950s motorcars, all made in Britain.

Wigan Heritage Service

Dating from just after the end of the Second World War, this picture shows Market Place looking towards Standishgate. Most of the buildings remain, though the ornate street lamps shown here are long gone. This view is particularly pleasing because it shows people going about their day to day activities without being affected by the camera. The public house on the right of the picture is the Old Dog Hotel, and Woolworths can be seen in the centre of the picture in premises now occupied by John Menzies the newsagents. Next to Woolworths the trusty Burtons building is visible. Station Road is the road which veers off to the right; how many local people would have travelled down there to catch their train to Manchester? Now, of course, most of the roadway in the scene has been transformed by the advent of pedestrianisation, which has taken the cars and their fumes out of the most central shopping areas in the town.

Wigan Heritage Service

A busy scene in Standishgate, looking north, and dating from the 1940s. It shows the prime site occupied by F.W.Woolworth (at the time of writing the premises are the local base of Menzies the newsagents) along with the Burton building and Marks and Spencers. Local people will notice the two Arcades located in this part of town, known to people as 'the Little Arcade' and the 'Big Arcade'.

This 1950s view of Library Street shows a variety of contemporary motor vehicles which set the scene in the picture, but the main building featured here is the Picturedrome Pavilion. The popular Wigan centre for entertainment was pulled down in the late 1950s and the site is now occupied by Wigan's swimming baths, a source of enjoyment of a different kind. During the construction of the baths workmen had, as you would expect, to dig down very deep in order to accommodate the pool. In the process they uncovered many artifacts from previous buildings on the site, which were of great interest to local archaeologists and historians. Looking up Library Street from the same standpoint today one can see a very similar view to this; the distinctive red walls of the Town Hall building look virtually the same, as do those of the ornate Municipal Buildings a little higher up the street, though the dome which characterised that building for so many years has long since gone.

Wigan Heritage Service

Wigan Heritage Service

This view was captured from the roof of the 'new' car park, looking down Chapel Lane. The main subjects of the photograph are the two cooling towers which were located at Westwood Power Station. The huge structures, each standing over 300 ft tall, were a well-known local landmark and could be seen from virtually every part of the town. The power station itself was constructed in 1950 but its useful life lasted less than forty years. Demolition of the cooling towers took place in 1989 and drew thousands of excited spectators to watch the event. Many people, particularly those who chose a vantage point a mile or two away from the towers, will recall the moment that the explosion took place; a cloud of smoke and a tremor could be detected at first, but no noise. Then, a tremendous explosion ripped through the air, causing photographers and observers alike to jump in the air with sheer surprise. The sound of cheering and applause followed, as the tension that had built up over the waiting minutes was released by the onlookers.

Wigan Markets - bringing bargains to shoppers for generations

Wigan Heritage Service

Wigan has been a 'market town' since the 13th century. The Royal Charter of 1246, which transformed the manor into a borough, confirmed the right to hold markets and fairs, which had been granted a short time earlier.

In 1246, after the charter was issued, an outdoor market was set up, located at Wallgate and Wigan has held open-air markets in the borough ever since.

Little is known of the presence of an indoor market before 1875 when preparations began to erect a new market hall. This decision came about after complaints by local road-users that the stalls which lined the streets were impeding traffic. To the infinite satisfaction of horse riders and pedestrians it was completed in 1877 at a total cost of £40,000 and officially opened on 21st May of that year. Wigan's old Market Hall was a spacious one storey building which was situated on Market Street.

It soon became a busy, thriving place. Food was fresh, cheap and often served by friends or family of the customer. The market hall enjoyed much popularity until it was demolished in 1988, bringing to an end over a century of Wigan's history. Nowadays the space is occupied by modern art galleries and a new private shopping complex.

Market Square (the area in front of the indoor market) did a booming trade in the first half of this century as Wigan's 'open-air' market, selling all kinds of produce, most of it from the carts and barrows of local farmers. People flocked to Market Square, believing the produce to be the cheapest in the North.

The former Market Hall was honoured by a Royal Visit in 1913, when King George V and Queen Mary arrived on 10th July. They were greeted by civic dignitaries on a specially erected Market Hall stage.

The authority now boasts, arguably the largest traditional markets service in the United Kingdom with over 750 stalls occupying seven sites around the borough. Markets have always been a speciality of the Borough and the Council operates one of he largest

market undertakings in the country. Wigan and Leigh, Ashton, Atherton, Golborne, Hindley and Tyldesley all boast thriving markets, offering rows of fresh fruit and veg to clothing for all, from books and records to the chance to snap up something a little more unusual.

Left: An unusual view of the indoor market hall in the 1940s. ***Below:*** *Womens magazines were clearly a massive part of the business operated from this stand in Wigan's indoor market hall. The picture dates from the late 1950s and features Smith's Newsagents. Mr Smith was famous in Wigan for his wealth of local knowledge and interest in everything to do with the history of the town. People looking at this picture may remember the popular cafe which was situated at the bottom left of the passage shown here, or, perhaps, the public house which was divided into two parts which was a favourite watering hole for many town centre drinkers.*

...tage Service

'That's another fine mess you've gotten me into..' could well be the caption to go with this picture. Wallgate Bridge under a foot of water was blocked to most forms of wheeled traffic when this photograph was taken in the 1930s. This area of Wigan was susceptible to flooding for many years, the cause being the nearby River Douglas which frequently spilled over its shallow banks, much to the inconvenience of local people. The bridge itself had a very distinctive advertisement for the Victoria Hotel which, according to the sign, offered 'first class accommodation and catering'. The Victoria Hotel in Wigan was established, next Wallgate railway station in 1894, two years before the station itself was opened. The hotel was built on the site of an earlier establishment of the same name.

Wigan Heritage Service

An interesting scene from the 1950s captured in Market Place and featuring a young point-duty policeman. Policemen would routinely work on point-duty in the days before virtually every major junction had traffic lights installed. Often a particular constable would work at the same junction for a number of years, and become known, at least by sight, to the hundreds of motorists who would pass by him every day. Traffic lights were first seen in Wigan in July 1930, located at the junction of Standishgate and the Mesnes Street Crossing. On the left of this photograph the popular family butchers 'Meadows' is well shaded to protect its meat products from the sun - but keen eyes and a magnifying glass can just make out a poster reading 'Ox Tongue - 1s 9d'.

Wallgate in 1969, and a trusty Leyland double decker makes its way towards a point-duty policeman standing opposite Library Street. The photograph seems quite modern, though it is over a quarter of a century old and contains several interesting characteristics from the period. Among the retail premises the wholesale tobacconists business run known as Ashton's can be seen, along with Johnston's the cleaners and the decorating store next door.

Northern Counties - building the country's buses since 1919

Wigan is famous for many things, not least of which being the construction of road-going public transport vehicles, though the vast majority of the travelling public outside the area is probably not aware of this. The town has been the base for several bus and coach body builders since the earliest days of the industry, though just one of these marques, Northern Counties, remains active today.

Northern Counties Motor and Engineering Company Limited was founded by Henry Gethin Lewis, a successful South Wales industrialist and colliery owner. The firm is still owned by the same family, the current chairman, Mr H.G. Lewis, being the son of the original founder. The company can trace its origins back to the first anniversary of the Armistice, 11th November 1919, when the records indicate that its first registered office was on Wigan Lane. The official documents record the nature of the company's business as being 'the construction of vehicle bodywork, carrying out motor vehicle repairs and the operation of a garage business'. Before long the company began to describe itself as 'body specialists'. By 1929 the registered office had moved to Mount Stuart Square in Cardiff, though the works remained, as they do today, at the current Wigan location.

Two large houses fronting onto Wigan Lane were later to become the firm's office block, and the gardens and orchards which once stood behind those houses are now the location of the works.

Specialisation

In the first few years after the business was established the firm built quality motor bodies for a wide variety of uses, for British as well as foreign

motor manufacturer's chassis. The arrival of the 1920s saw Northern Counties firmly established as a manufacturer of public vehicle bodies, and, at this time they were all single-deck by nature. By 1923 the bus and charabanc business had grown to such an extent that car body construction ceased altogether, though the occasional one-off commission for hearses etc. would still be fitted in around the public service vehicle work.

Unlike modern motor manufacturing, Northern Counties took pride in the claim that every element of motor body construction, such as body panel manufacture, wood work, painting, special component fabrication and upholstering etc. was carried out by the firm's own craftsmen. This meant that quality standards could be maintained at the

highest levels because all the activities were under the company's own strict control. The company soon built a reputation as a major force in the bus and coach body world, and went on to build its first double-decker body in 1928. Later, in 1933, Northern Counties passed another milestone with the construction of their first steel-framed double decked body, and in doing so became one of the first manufacturers to adopt this progressive method of construction. During their long history Northern Counties have concentrated on the construction of service buses in preference to coaches, though a handful of exceptions to this rule are recorded. Overall, however, the firm is known throughout the public transport industry for its fine contribution to service buses, and has no prouder time in its history than the vehicles it turned out in the dark days of the war. During the Second World War the company was tasked with building utility bodies for a small number of operators who were desperate for vehicles. Most were double deckers, almost all of which were built on Daimler or Guy chassis. In order to save precious raw materials the upper decks would some-times be of timber constr-

uction. Other wartime assignments included the building of general purpose truck bodies for use on Albion chassis and the assembly of motorcycles and trucks provided by the U.S.A as part of the 'lease-lend' scheme.

Many unusual vehicles were been produced by the company in the years during, and shortly after the war. A three-wheeled ambulance based on a Scammell 'Mechanical Horse' was one concept which never really caught on. Rail cars for the Clogher Valley Railway in Northern Ireland, and for Brazil and Peru were immediate post-war projects. Many other foreign countries such as Hong Kong and Denmark have also taken delivery of the Wigan firm's vehicles. The firm was involved in the development of prototype electric vans with Lucas and the Post Office in the 1970s.

Massey Brothers join the fold

In 1967 the company was continuing to grow; demand for the firm's vehicle bodies was buoyant, and the fully-developed site had no capacity for expansion. The opportunity to acquire another Wigan bus body builder arose at this time, and the firm, Massey Brothers Ltd., was a perfect addition to the existing operation. The Massey works, at

Pemberton, is three miles from the Wigan Lane site, and concentrates on the final fitting of windows, seats and upholstery, as well as final trimming and painting.

The quality of vehicles supplied by Northern Counties is well known throughout the industry. The steel frame and pillar construction gives the bodies tremendous strength, an important characteristic in these safety-conscious days. The firm has always been noted and respected for its ability to deliver products tailored to the client's exact specifications, no matter how large or small the order. Many one-off vehicles exist which are keenly sought by bus enthusiasts all around the the country, and beyond.

After the Management Buyout in August 1992 the company was subsequently sold to the Henly's Group Plc in May 1995, joining Henly's other bus manufacturer, Plaxton Coach & Bus, in their Bus Manufacturing Division.

Today, as the Northern Counties approaches its eightieth year in business the company is confident of the contribution it can make to the future of the public transport industry. As the trend

towards fast, clean and efficient public transport systems gathers momentum it is predicted that the requirements and expectations of the travelling public will increase. This can only be good news for Northern Counties, a company which has built a solid reputation on its ability to stay ahead of the competition by skillfully anticipating the needs of its customers.

Facing page: A late 1920s view of the bodyshop with examples of Ford, Austin, Vauxhall and Moon chassis awaiting the attention of the bodybuilders.
This page, above: A 1927 Karrier operated by Wigan Corporation. This vehicle had brakes on the rear wheels only, although with a maximum permitted speed of 12 mph, this was probably an adequate arrangement!
Below: An aerial view of the Northern Counties site at Pemberton, giving an idea of its substantial size.

A local firm's success story that began just after the war...

The story of Ratcliffe's, the well known Ashton-in-Makerfield company, goes back to the early 1950s. John William Ratcliffe, known to most people as Bill Ratcliffe, started the firm after working for many years as a pit engineer. His engineering skills were well developed in the mining industry, but Bill had ambitions to do more for himself and his family, and was keen to find an area of business which would exploit his entrepreneurial instincts as well as the talent for engineering he had acquired.

Supply and Demand

The early 1950s, only a few years after the end of the war, were austere in almost every respect of life and commerce throughout Britain. Demand, in many areas was not matched by supply, and transport was no exception.

Rebuilding the country after the war, and getting Britain back on her industrial feet, would depend upon transportation, and it was not yet possible to supply enough new vehicles to satisfy the needs of development businesses.

There were, however, massive numbers of ex-Ministry of Defence vehicles which, in these post-war years were surplus to requirements. The vehicles available were tremendously variable in terms of their condition and suitability for use by private companies. Crucially, they could be obtained at very reasonable prices and Bill Ratcliffe was quick to see an opportunity here.

Putting his engineering skills to good use, Bill started a company with the aim of refurbishing and converting ex M.O.D. trucks for use by eager customers. The business thrived, thanks largely to Bill Ratcliffe's reputation for honesty and fairness, shrewd buying and the quality of the conversions which was made possible by the years of engineering craftsmanship which Bill had acquired.

Haulage

As the firm grew, the nature of the business made it sensible to move into the related field of haulage. This move took place only a few years after Bill Ratcliffe had taken the bold move to start out on his own, and the results soon began to show that he had made a wise choice.

The first signs of the recovery of British industry in the 1950s caused a healthy demand for road haulage services and the firm soon found a ready market for their increasing fleet of tippers and flat-backed lorries. Major early contracts are remembered with fondness; carrying loads of salt and sand for local industry and hinges and fittings for a local company, Thomas Crompton, travelling from Cornwall to the North of Scotland. It is a sobering thought to remember that at this time not one mile of motorway existed in Britain, and that the lorries of the time

Trevor Ratcliffe, busily cleaning an S Type Bedford lorry in the early 1960s.

injection equipment was was becoming an increasingly common feature of modern commercial vehicle engines.

Family ties

In the mid-1960s Bill's two sons, Trevor and Alan, joined the business straight from school, learning the business from top to bottom from their father as well as other experienced members of the successful company. In the the mid 1970s the company sold its transport interests and moved into the property field, setting up as Trevalan Estates. Bill worked actively in the business until

Trevor Ratcliffe, flanked by Austin, Bedford and Ford lorries in the 1960s.

The company has always taken pride in the livery of its fleet

his death in 1994, at the age of seventy three. The vast experience of haulage and storage gained in the early years of the company has not been lost; in 1977 Trevor set up his own business in the transport and storage field. Modern times have seen the property interests pursued by the firm flourish, but even these have close connections with the truck and motor industry upon which the firm has its foundations. Storage yards and a car auction site were bought and developed in 1987, and the vehicle side of the business remains a small, but valued aspect of current activities.

When Bill Ratcliffe started his business half a century ago, his modest ambitions for the firm were based on a belief that an honest, fair and hard working approach to commerce would ensure success. Fifty years on, it is clear that this approach has paid off.

were much slower and less comfortable than the ones which today's drivers enjoy.

The truck-conversion side of the business continued alongside the growing haulage activity. In the late 1960s, when the Crompton's contract ended, the firm decided to expand it's work in the field of commercial vehicle sales. In tandem with this, a vehicle and trailer hire service was established which incorporated the repair and service of the fuel

The Ratcliffe fleet in the 1950s. Unlike today, most lorries on the road were British made

WAR WEAPONS WEEK

£250,000

OUR AIM THIS WEEK.....

Wigan Heritage Service

War Weapons Week was part of a series of fund-raising campaigns which took place throughout Britain during the Second World War. Their object was to encourage people and businesses to invest in War Bonds, not to donate their money with no hope of ever seeing it again, and Local Savings Committees were set up throughout the country to give the drive real impetus. The photograph shown here relates to Wigan's War Weapons Week which took place from November 30th to December 7 1940, the initial aim of which was to raise £250,000.

Part of the activities included a march past and military parade which involved the Lancashire Fusiliers, a detachment of artillery, the Saint John's Ambulance Brigade, The WVS, the Red Cross and other locally-represented organisations. The salute was taken by the Regional

Commissioner of the A.R.P, Sir Harry Haigh, standing, with other dignitaries on a platform outside the Market Hall.

War Weapons Week proved hugely successful; even by today's standards the amount of money raised seems phenomenal, with £180,000 being raised by the end of the first day! The week had been inaugurated by the Mayor, Alderman J H Banks JP who said that he was proud to be associated with the the aim of the campaign and that it had the object of linking all classes who had the desire to put an end to the 'horrible massacre of human beings'.

Soon the £250,000 mark had been passed and the aim was then to double the total by the end of the week; Wigan people were gripped by the exercise and money flooded in from every available source. Wigan Corporation invested £25,000 and the total exceeded three times the original target, with £815,000 being raised for the war effort prompting a letter of thanks and congratulations to be sent by the Prime Minister, Winston Churchill to the people of Wigan.

A campaign in 1941 to raise money for Warships enabled Wigan to adopt the Destroyer HMS

Wigan Heritage Service

Wigan Heritage Service

Janus, a ship which was sunk by the enemy in 1944.

In 1942 a ten week campaign was organised to raise money for tanks, and Wigan raised £228,000 which was sufficient to purchase five Churchill Tanks which were named in her honour. The following year saw the people of Wigan raise £650,000 in aid of Wings for Victory Week.

The photographs on this page show workers from the Beech Hill Munitions factory. They took part in the Parade which took place on the Monday of War Weapons Week. Generally the girls enjoyed their work at Beech Hill; it was a chance to earn what has been described as 'good money' - much better than they were used to during peacetime, and have secure employment, which again would have been new to them. Overtime was paid, in fact, required at the works, and the girls enjoyed a good social life too. Tommy Handley once visited the works and performed in the canteen which acted as a makeshift concert hall on the day.

Left: This startling picture dates from Thursday December 5 1940 and depicts a captured German bomber. The aeroplane had been put on public view in Wigan as part of a fund-raising campaign with the catchy title *War Weapons Week* which was organised by the Local Savings Committee. The scene is unmistakably Market Square; the combination of the wet granite cobbles underfoot, the imposing red brick building of O & C Rushton Ltd, known universally by Wiganers as the *Gas Showrooms*, and the Nazi bomber itself, paint a vivid picture of the atmosphere which pervaded the area in the early years of the war.

Wigan Heritage Service

Right: This *Ford Emergency Food Van* was one of a large number supplied free of charge to the people of Britain in wartime by Henry Ford and his son, Edsel. This example, registration number JNO 303 was maintained by H. Williams & Co. Ltd of Wallgate, and formed part of a wider contingency organised by the Civil Defence Emergency Sub-Committee of the Borough Council. Every local cafe owner, hotelier and factory canteen manager in the Wigan area was requested to attend a meeting in December 1940 to determine a strategy for 'mass feeding' should Wigan be devastated by an enemy attack. At the meeting the catering experts handed over lists of their equipment and facilities, estimating the number of people they considered able to feed in the event of an emergency. Wigan already had access to two mobile 'caravan-style' canteens, but no spare vehicles to tow them. An application by the Chief Constable for two motor cars was approved by the Corporation in 1940, and the Town Clerk wrote to the Minister of Health for a grant to cover the emergency expenses. Wigan's wartime feeding contingency was up and running.

Wigan Heritage Service

Right: In wartime Wigan, as in the rest of the country, many things were rationed in order to ensure that everyone would have at least enough food to survive, now that imported supplies were curtailed as a result of attacks on shipping. At the start, rationing was based upon weights of food allowable per person per week. These were: 4oz bacon/ham, 12oz sugar, 2oz tea, and 4oz butter. In addition, meat to the value of 1s 10d (9 new pence) per adult could be purchased per week. Every eight weeks each adult was entitled to a ration of dried egg which was the equivalent of 12 fresh eggs.

As the Germans became more successful in their campaign to disrupt the import of food from abroad with their U-Boat activity it became necessary to extend rationing to other types of food. Eventually, virtually everything you can think of was affected, including: rice, tomatoes, fish, canned meat, biscuits, peas, sago, syrup and many other foodstuffs. In Wigan there was an Emergency food Depot situated on Woodhouse Lane. Schoolchildren were provided with one hot meal per day, plus free milk under the National Milk Scheme. For the under-twos there was free cod-liver oil and blackcurrent juice. All part of the national plan to ensure that a balanced diet was available capable of keeping the nation healthy and as free as possible from disease.

8th June, 1946

TO-DAY AS WE CELEBRATE VICTORY

I send this personal message to you and all other boys and girls at school. For you have shared in the hardships and dangers of a total war and you have shared no less in the triumph of the Allied Nations.

I know you will always feel proud to belong to a country which was capable of such supreme effort; proud, too, of parents and elder brothers and sisters who by their courage, endurance and enterprise brought victory. May these qualities be yours as you grow up and join in the common effort to establish among the nations of the world unity and peace.

George R.I.

DISTRIBUTED in the SCHOOLS of the COUNTY BOROUGH of WIGAN

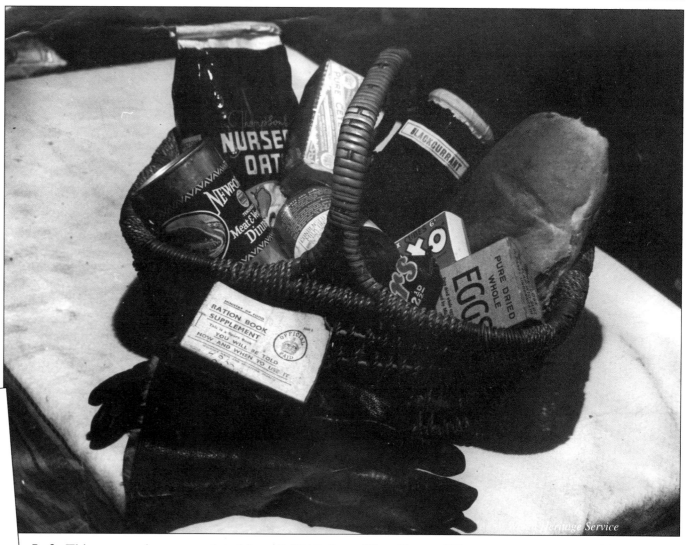

Wigan Heritage Service

Left: This personal message dated June 8 1946, from King George VI was sent to every pupil at Wigan's schools to mark the end of the Second World War. The King had made a special wireless broadcast at the end of the War on Monday 7 May 1945, declaring as he did so that the day after would be V.E Day, signifying victory in Europe. Nowhere were the celebrations more vigorous or heartfelt than in Wigan; the town was decked out in red white and blue flags and bunting. The Parish Church bells which had been silent since 1939 rang out every hour from early on V.E Day until late at night. There were fireworks and bonfires, with the inevitable burning of life-size dummies representing Hitler. Everyone in Wigan was celebrating the end of the most challenging period that most of them could remember, celebrations tinged with a certain degree of sadness, but celebrations nevertheless.

Many changes have taken place in this part of town since this photograph was taken the year after the end of the war, in August 1946. The picture is beautifully composed, with the familiar clock tower of the Parish Church peeping over the rooftops. Many of the retailers shown in the picture will be familiar to more mature readers; Lee's Cafe, Fletchers and the Olde Dog Hotel on the left hand side of the picture, and Hunter's Chemists, Waterworth's Florists and Bolton's the ironmongers on the right hand side of the street. In the centre of the picture we can see Victoria House, the location of the much-loved department store known as Lowe's. Note the lovely ornate lamp standards which blend so well with the tudor-style buildings in the photograph. The atmosphere is completed by the nostalgic effect brought about by the double decker bus, the stern-faced lorry and the curvaceous motorcar in the picture. Pure nostalgia!

Wigan Heritage Service

Bedding plants, on sale outside the Market Hall in 1951 proved to be a big draw, attracting hundreds of people to the location. From the expression on the gentleman's face you can tell that he really doesn't appreciate having his picture taken, though his wife (who is the image of my own grandmother by the way) is far too engrossed in the business of plant purchasing to bother about that. Preston's the furnishers and the premises of WHS Taylor & Co., the Depot for 'Harvest Home' pure food and Good Cheer Tea can be seen in the background.

If this picture fails to bring back memories of market trading in Wigan then nothing else will! There has been a tradition of selling produce from the back of open trucks, and before they existed, the back of horse-drawn carts. All kinds of claims have been made in local history books about the market selling the cheapest farm produce of anywhere in Lancashire, brought in by farmers from the surrounding district. The lovely classic lorries pictured here are reminiscent of the ones featured in old British films; you can almost hear the whining axles and crunching gearboxes when you look at them here. Note the three-wheeled commercial vehicle on the left of the picture - possibly an early Commer and long since disappeared from our roads. Each of these commercial vehicles seemed to have a personality and individuality that is lacking in their modern equivalents. On the right of the picture, the open rear platforms of a pair of Wigan double decker buses is just visible, alongside the distinctive curved kerbside of the old bus station.

Wigan Heritage Service

Victoria House was the home of the popular department store owned and operated by Lowe's. This photograph, thought to date from the late 1950s, shows the front of the store from the direction of Market Place. Many, perhaps more mature Wiganers will have fond memories of the cafe, located upstairs in the store; it was a popular meeting place, and widely regarded as the place to be and be seen in by local people. The demolition of the building was considered to be a sad occasion by Wigan shoppers, though there was one silver lining for townsfolk which should not go unmentioned; for as long as people could remember it had been impossible to get a view of the Parish Church from a reasonable distance, simply as a result of the proximity of the surrounding buildings. During the time that Victoria House had been cleared, and before the modern building which replaced it had been constructed, local people could view and photograph the church in a new light.

Rigby's was a household name in Wigan for well over a century and a quarter. The family firm which specialised in boots and shoes was established in 1835, two years before Queen Victoria came to the throne, in a small shop located on Wigan Lane. Several years later, the firm outgrew its first premises and moved to a larger shop on Wallgate. This picture features Rigby's later store which was situated at Library Street. It is thought to date from the mid 1950s and shows the distinctive and very imposing Rigby's sign topped off with ornate ironwork, which will bring back memories for many Wigan folk who used to patronise the popular store. With a reputation for high quality and good service, the business thrived until the 1970s when the last descendent of the founder involved in the business retired, sadly meaning that another small indepedent local retailer passed into the realms of history. The premises are now occupied by a well-known Building Society.

Wigan Heritage Service

Edwards Bakery - over a century of baking fit for Royalty

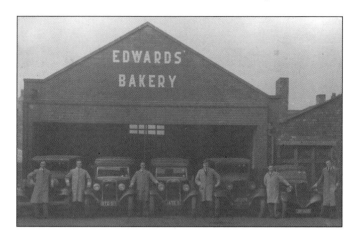

After 100 years, Edwards Bakery has the distinction of being the only one in Wigan which is still managed and operated by descendants of the founding family.

It is a success story which started in tragic circumstances; In the 19th century, Cornish miners travelled all over the country, selling their skills. One family settled in Platt Bridge but the head of the household, Mr Edwards, a shaft sinker died in 1892, leaving his widow, Anne with a young family. At this time there were no widow's pensions - and no welfare for miners. There was, however, the Poor Law, and with it the threat of the Workhouse in Frog Lane.

Inspired by this, Anne started making pies in her little fireside oven, and she and her children went out selling them. Anne eventually remarried a local man called Tom Ashurst. The growing business kept the Edwards name through William, Anne's son by her first marriage.

The bakery was further developed by James in the 1930s, and 40s, helped by his wife, Gladys. The future of Edwards' Bakery is set to continue

through Andrew and Duncan, sons of the present directors, William and Alan.

It still provides customers with quality products, because some of the secrets of baking excellence which began in Anne's fireside oven are still in use. An Edwards' cake was chosen, in the early 1990s, for the Queen Mother's Birthday Awards in London,

specially baked by Duncan, a qualified chef in the Platt Bridge Bakery.

Entering its second century, Edwards' Bakery continues to make oven-fresh products, not just for shops but for a variety of social functions and venues. It also supplies cold meats, such as their own roast ham, topside and turkey, cheeses and all the other 'goodies' required for any successful celebration.

Above: *Princess Diana visiting an Edwards shop in the early 1990s.* **Far left:** *This picture dates from 1938 and shows the Edwards Bakery staff.* **Left:** *James Edwards, celebrating after winning an award for Currant Bread making in the 1940s.*

Highams Florists - bringing colour to Wigan since 1910

demand. By the 1930s the business was operating from no less than four different locations; Market Veranda, 18 Darlington Street and 22 Makinson Arcade, as well as from the original base at 119 Darlington Street East.

The Second World War

The outbreak of war saw many changes in Wigan, German bombs were always a threat and the Higham's shop at 22 Makinson Arcade was designated an A.R.P basement air-raid shelter capable of giving respite to 42 citizens in the event of an enemy attack. All six sons went to war and unusually, all six came home alive and well.

Today

Higham's Florists are held in high esteem by the people of Wigan; florists touch the lives of families at times when they are experiencing the extremes of emotion - the birth of a child, weddings of friends and families, those important anniversaries and celebrations, not forgetting the sadder times when consolation may be found from the expression of support and sympathy that only flowers can bring.

The early days

Mention flowers in Wigan, and most people will immediately think of the name 'Highams'. The family-run florists have been a major player in Wigan's world of floristry for almost a century.

Darlington Street East

The business was established in 1910 by Florence and Henry Higham, the parents of William Higham from whom the firm takes its name. Initially the business was based at 119 Darlington Street East in Wigan, where the family made their living selling fruit, vegetables and, of course, flowers. Florence and Henry had six sons and two daughters, all of whom were born and raised in Darlington Street East. As their reputation grew, so did the success of the business, and it was not long before more premises were acquired to satisfy the burgeoning

Almost a century of quality service

As Higham's Florists approach one hundred years of service to the people of Wigan it is fascinating to ponder on just how many scores of thousands of lives have been brightened and enriched by this

Wigan institution working quietly, almost behind the scenes in the Makinson Arcade.

Above: *Florence Higham (daughter of the founders) taken in the 1920s, outside of the Darlington Street premises.*

Facing page: *Florence and James Higham (son and daughter of the founders) taken in the 1920s.*

Above, right: *A display dating from 1980.*

The History Shop

Library Street, Wigan WN1 1NU
Telephone: **01942 828128**

New from 1996

The Charter Exhibition celebrating Wigan's 750th Charter Anniversary
The Charter Mural
New Art Gallery
A tribute to Rev William Wickham

Also

* Audio-visual theatre
* 'Founded on Coal' - the story of the area
* Temporary exhibition programme
* Research centre for local and family history
* Shop - quality 'heritage' goods
* School class visits
* Monthly lecture programme
* 'Past Forward' - Wigan Heritage Service's free newsletter

Opening Times
Monday: 10.00 - 7.00
Tues - Fri: 10.00 - 5.00
Saturday: 10.00 - 1.00

Other Heritage Service attractions
Archives Service, Leigh
Local History, Leigh
Astley Green Colliery

Wigan Heritage Service

This picture reveals just how much the act of shopping has changed over the years. This photograph is over sixty years old and has an almost museum-like appearance. There are tell-tale clues as to the ethos which underpinned 1930s retailing practices; most obviously the presence of a chair - a minor point but evidence that shopkeepers in the 1930s were not simply interested in taking your money and getting you out of the door. In those days it seems that people had more time for each other, and that personal service meant just that. Another clue to the era featured here include the immaculate glass barriers along the front of the counter to prevent eager little hands touching the merchandise - and the shiny metal weighing scales which would have been put to frequent use.

H. Plumb & Son - a 'sound vision' that paid off!

On the 16th October 1945 H Plumb & Son was established as an electrical distributor by Mr Harry Plumb at number 1A Dicconson Street, Wigan. Three years later Ron Plumb, Harry's son, entered the business as a part time member of staff and electrical engineer.

The business went from strength to strength over the following decade and in 1960 a three storey terraced house on Dicconson Street was purchased and converted, to provide storage facilities and a further service department repairing radios, televisions and domestic appliances.

When stereo recording was invented in the late 1960s, it brought with it a completely new age of sound equipment and the company seized the opportunity to sell stereo radiograms and audio systems.

1967 was a good year for the company. Firstly, it won orders from local hospitals to design, build and install new hospital radio equipment and following this success it built a new hi-fi showroom on the corner of Dicconson Street and Standishgate, incorporating all the ideas of modern shop design and the latest technical innovations.

That same year the company was appointed the Sony dealership and the following year Bang and Olufsen awarded it the same honour.

When colour television was invented in 1970 H Plumb & Son had customers queuing out of the doors for the new invention. Demand exceeded supply and some customers had to wait weeks for their product. Following their success with the hospital radio equipment in 1967, H Plumb & Son helped to develop a communication system for the

The original premises of H Plumb & Son, taken in 1968

world famous Charnely Theatre for their work on hip surgery. Later that year, the company supplied and operated a public address system for the Prime Minister, Harold Wilson's visit to Wigan.

In 1972 Harry Plumb retired, leaving the business in the capable hands of his son, Ron who showed his father's initiative almost immediately by moving to a brand new shop in Standishgate, bringing with it a completely new style of clean, quality retailing. A purpose built service department was opened on the outskirts of the town which catered for the ever growing customer demand.

Over the next few years Ron Plumb decided to broaden the company's horizons and after scouting round for an ideal location he chose Leigh and opened a second branch. In 1974 H Plumb & Son formed a Limited Company. A third branch was opened in 1977 at Mealhouse Lane, Bolton.

Plumb's expertise was rewarded many times over the next few years. The company was awarded Bang & Olufsen dealer of the year in 1977 and was awarded official supplier of televisions to both Wigan and St Helens Education Committees. Two years later it won the contract to supply all Lancashire County Council establishments.

The start of the 1980s brought a wave of change throughout the country and the name H Plumb & Son was changed to Plumbs as a reflection of the more modern times.

By the mid 1980s branches at Bury, Warrington and Chorley had been added to the company, followed in 1984 by a branch at St Helens in the prestigious new Hardshaw Shopping Centre.

Over the following decade the company opened more branches at Southport and Altrincham, as well as modernisation to some of the existing stores. A new state of the art computer system was installed and Plumbs embarked on a programme to achieve BS 5750 to improve its customer service even further.

In 1996 Plumbs moved the Wigan Standishgate shop after 26 years of trading there....to next door, into premises twice the size to meet the needs of a growing product range.

WHATEVER CHANGES, YOU CAN ALWAYS RELY ON PLUMBS

Since our first shop opened for business in Wigan in 1946, TV and audio equipment has changed more than a little.

Walk in to any of Plumbs branches now though, and you'll find that's all that's changed.

As we did all those years ago, we stock the latest developments in TV and audio technology.

Our staff are just as friendly and helpful as ever. And we still attach great importance to making sure every customer gets superb service.

Call in to Plumbs soon. We guarantee you'll find it a refreshing change.

BRANCHES THROUGHOUT THE NORTH WEST

ALTRINCHAM • BOLTON • BURY • CHORLEY • LEIGH • SOUTHPORT •
ST.HELENS • WARRINGTON • WIGAN

Plumbs
sound & vision centres

MARKETGATE

Shopping Centre
Wigan

Ready to shop? Then Marketgate is your first stop!

A warm Wigan welcome awaits you!

The Marketgate Shopping Centre has been established for many years and has grown in stature as one of Wigan's most pleasant, vibrant and convenient places to shop and socialise. For the benefit of our customers the Centre is linked to a 650 space car park.

Offering a range of famous brand names, speciality shops, ladies, mens and childrens fashions, books, sportswear, TV, video, electronics as well as an excellent coffee shop, Marketgate is shopping at its best - in the heart of the town centre.

Market Place, Wigan, Lancashire WN1 1JS   Tel 01942 236139 Fax 01942 826276

70,000 people a week can't be wrong!

Marketgate Shopping Centre, old fashioned values in a modern setting

Hunter's Chemist shop taken in the late 1940s. The Marketgate Shopping Centre was later built on part of this site.

Conveniently situated right in the heart of Wigan's thriving shopping area, Marketgate is the exciting, forward-looking jewel in the crown of the town's retail activities. The clean, stylish facilites which characterise Marketgate form a unique blend with Wigan's traditional architectural style - an achievement which is the surely the envy of many other towns central shopping facilities. The last two decades have seen the remarkable transformation of the shopping facilities in the area. Marketgate is an integral part of the overall improvements which have succeeded in attracting shoppers from well beyond the boundaries of the Metropolitan Borough. Marketgate itself was once considered to be a rather uninspiring example of a 1960s shopping mall, though today's shoppers could never acuse it of being dull.

On the present site of the Marketgate Shopping Centre a small arcade, known by many as the 'Legs of Man' after the pub at the top of the arcade. During the 1970s the arcade was modernised and renamed as the Wigan Centre Arcade. As time went by it became a very popular shopping area and attracted a further bout of revevelopment and refurbishment in the 1980s. This time, a mock tudor facade was incorporated in the design so that it would blend in with the surrounding buildings for which Wigan has become well known. From this time the popular shopping facility became known as Marketgate.

The success of Marketgate in attracting over 70,000 shoppers every week is known and appreciated by the retailers and traders who run their thriving businesses from the location. The reason for the success of the centre has much to do with the quality of the retailing establishments based there, and the range, diversity and quality of the products which are on offer at Marketgate.

The adjacent open and covered market areas are tremendously popular, and all the facilities at Marketgate are just a short walk away from convenient town-centre car parks and the modern bus station. Shoppers may also take advantage of Marketgate's charming coffee shop; a few minutes break from the shopping expedition in the most pleasant of surroundings. Some of them, no doubt, reflecting on how things have changed over the years in Wigan, but thankful nevertheless that there is still a place where they can indulge in the art of 'proper shopping'. The unsung heroes working in the shops and behind the scenes at the centre can be relied upon to make this possible for many years to come.

Coops building lives on

The early days
In the 1860s Wigan was one of the many Lancashire towns which prospered greatly from the production of cotton with its other main industry being coal.

Following the outbreak of the American Civil War the cotton and coal industries suffered badly when sources of the raw material were prevented from being exported.

Public-spirited
Mr Timothy Coop, who was a retail tailor in Wigan, served upon a Relief Committee which aimed to raise funds to provide relief for the unemployed in the area. He formed the idea of teaching the unemployed women of Wigan to sew and be employed in the manufacture of gentlemen's clothing.

Dorning Street
He built up the business gradually and secured a large plot of land in Dorning Street, in order to build suitable premises to meet the rapidly increasing trade. On 4th March 1872 the building was officially opened. The original factory building is the current right hand section. In 1888 and 1890 two new wings were added to extend the original factory. A new front entrance was formed in the centre. The top (fifth) floor of the right hand section was demolished in the 1980s to lessen internal structural problems within that part of the building.

Phoenix from the ashes
Timothy Coop and Company was a major employer in the town until 1989 when the factory closed. Purchased by the Grosvenor Housing Association it was decided to maintain the original ideals of Timothy Coop. It seems fitting that a building which first opened in 1871 to give work to the unemployed now provides a valuable resource to improve the employment prospects of young people.

Restoration
Major refurbishment has now taken place, offering accommodation for single people, as well as a resource room which aims to help the unemployed back into the job market, Coops bridges the gap between young people leaving home and setting up alone.

The restoration has taken place sympathetically to ensure that a building which has stood proud in Wigan town centre for 125 years and is held in high esteem by local people will continue to serve the town.

Mornington High School

Serving the Community

Mornington Road, Hindley, Wigan WN2 4LG
Tel: 01942 767704 Fax: 01942 748054

Mornington High School

A progressive school with strong traditions

Beginnings

Mornington High School began life at Argyle Street in the early 1900s. It was a Central School in the early years of this century.

The school catered for pupils over eleven and although it wasn't a secondary school it was moving away from elementary education. It had two divisions, as was the nature of the day: boys and girls were educated separately. It only became a mixed school in the 1940s.

Post War Changes

At the end of the Second World War the school became a secondary modern and in 1955 was renamed Hindley County Secondary School, part of Lancashire Division 14. Mr J Lowe, a well known Hindley man was Headteacher from 1953 - 1980.

The school grew progressively over the years and before long it became apparent that a larger, more appropriate site was necessary. After searching for an ideal location the school moved in January 1967 to its present site at Mornington Road and changed its name again to Mornington High School.

During the days of the transfer the Argyle Street site was retained for the first year pupils and for many years afterwards.

The school was one of the first secondary modern schools in Wigan to develop GCE 'O' Level courses for pupils who had failed the 11+. The school established a strong tradition in this field.

Expansion

The school expanded rapidly over the following years and at its largest was educating around 1300 pupils with over 70 teaching staff. With the abolition of the 11+, the school developed a comprehensive intake in the 1970s.

Today

Mornington is now the only secondary school located in Hindley. A comprehensive school, it offers a full range of GCSE courses to 1050 pupils. The school has also become a community school and provides community classes and leisure activities during evenings and weekends, seven days a week for 800 adults.

ABRAHAM GUEST HIGH SCHOOL

'FIAT LUX'
translation:
'OPEN YOUR EYES TO LEARNING'

Abraham Guest High School aims to do just that by providing pupils with the ideas, skills, information and training which will enable them to make full use of their leisure time and be able to earn their living when they enter the world of work.

We acknowledge that we cannot achieve these aims by ourselves so we actively encourage the involvement of staff, pupils, parents, community and industry in the vital process of education.

ADULT CENTRE

We offer:

- A wide range of social and academic evening classes throughout the year
- IT facilities including word processing, Data Bases and Spread Sheet facilities, Corel draw, Aldus Pagemaker & Colour Scanner
- Lettings of our sports facilities to local teams
- Hiring of rooms for conferences, meetings, fund raising activities etc.

For more information on any of our services please contact:
Mr K Massey or
Miss S Stockley
on 01942 225543

Open your eyes to learning

Abraham Guest High School was officially opened on 5th October 1960 by Dame Mary Smieton OBE, the permanent secretary at the Ministry of Education at that time. Originally, the school was designed to cater for 370 children from the Lamberhead Green and Holgate County primary schools. With a growing reputation for excellence Abraham Guest High School now takes in pupils from a much wider area.

The school was named after County Alderman Abraham Guest who died in April 1957 at the age of 84. Alderman Guest had been heavily involved in education in the area, serving as the Chairman on Wigan & District Mining and Technology College governing body. His brother was the Director of Education. The school crest includes a stag's head and a sceptre which were respectively part of the coats of arms of the Stanley and Bispham families who at one time were lords of the manor. The motto 'Fiat Lux', freely translated, means 'Let there be light' although the school places an educational emphasis on its translation, 'Open your eyes to learning'.

Located in the Winstanley ward, Abraham Guest serves the Orrell and Billinge areas as well. Close links with its community are reflected in the popularity of the school, namely the extensive use of the facilities during evenings and weekends. A School Inspectors report concluded: "Abraham Guest is a good school with some excellent features. It deserves the high regard in which it is held by parents".

SOME RELATIONSHIPS

ARE BUILT

TO LAST

At Mercedes-Benz the philosophy has always been 'das beste oder nichts': the best or nothing.

Indeed the reliability of Mercedes engineering is legendary. And once you experience the smoothness, the solid feel and precise handling of a Mercedes you will never be satisfied with anything else, which is perhaps why many of our customers buy a Mercedes again.

There are models to suit every individual need. So why not telephone us and book a test drive today? At HL Gorner you will find that our service is just like our cars: designed to last.

Our commitment to every aspect of the service provided will enhance the pleasure of owning one of the **Best Cars in the World.**

Milner Street, Warrington WA5 1AD Tel 01925 570057
Wigan Road, Ashton-in-Makerfield, Wigan WN4 8LY Tel 01942 717373
Old Road, Clapham, via Lancaster LA2 8JG Tel 015242 51000

Mercedes-Benz

Over 60 years of service to the motorist

From humble beginnings, repairing cars in a small wooden building in the 1930s, Horace Gorner nurtured the business which has grown into the largest independent Mercedes-Benz dealership in the region.

The company is now run by the second and third generation of the Gorner family who maintain the tradition of superb service, personal care and attention to detail.

A 1950s picture of the H L Gorner site with a Standard Vanguard in front of the workshop.

In 1962 H L Gorner became agents for Rootes cars and a new showroom replaced the old wooden building on the same site in Ashton-in-Makerfield, on the outskirts of Wigan. Rootes were taken over by Chrysler who were later taken over by Talbot, but the only changes made at H L Gorner were those relating to their continued expansion. 1966 saw the building of a brand new showroom, parts department and workshop facility. Ten years later, with a firmly established reputation as a fair and approachable dealer, H L Gorner took another giant step forward to become a Mercedes-Benz main dealer.

In 1986 the company acquired a second Mercedes-Benz dealership in the picturesque Yorkshire Dales and H L Gorner, Clapham, was born. Bearing in mind the demands of a rural community, H L Gorner, Clapham diversified into the 'off road' market in 1991, becoming an agent for Daihatsu as well as Mercedes.

The Clapham site also includes a Light Commercial dealership. Clapham is under the management of General Manager Kevin Monk who, until his promotion in 1986, was sales manager at Wigan.

H L Gorner's excellent reputation for commitment to quality was further enhanced in 1993 when they were awarded the quality assurance management system standard BS5750 Part II, which has since become European standard BS EN ISO 9002.

In 1994, with two Mercedes dealerships and a Daihatsu dealership already to their credit, H L Gorner opened a third Mercedes-Benz dealership in Warrington. This new dealership is comprehensively equipped to attend to customers' requirements for new and used car sales, service and parts sales, with the back up of the body and paint facility at Wigan.

November 1996 saw the start of a £1.5 million investment in the re-development of the original site in Ashton-in-Makerfield. Due for completion in mid 1997, the new look dealership will include a state of the art 30 car showroom, a conservatory-style TV/coffee lounge, a smaller second lounge and a unique Mercedes-Benz boutique selling an array of gifts, clothing and accessories. Brand new offices, administration areas, a refurbished parts department, plus computer and telephone equipment specially designed to link the three sites, complete the redevelopment which represents the largest investment in the firm's history.

In 1997 H L Gorner also celebrates 21 years with the Mercedes-Benz franchise but, despite their obvious success, H L Gorner never forget their humble beginnings. Customers today are still assured of the highest quality of service and personal care, the solid foundations on which the company is built.

A late 1960s Humber Sceptre on the left and a Singer Vogue on the right hand side of the workshop.